TRAIN
LEAVES THE
STATION

Bill Martin Jr, Ph.D., has devoted his life to the education of young children. *Bill Martin Books* reflect his philosophy: that children's imaginations are opened up through the play of language, the imagery of illustration, and the permanent joy of reading books.

Published by The Trumpet Club
666 Fifth Avenue, New York, New York 10103

Text copyright © 1988 by Eve Merriam
Illustrations copyright © 1992 by Dale Gottlieb

The poem "Train Leaves the Station" was previously published in 1988 by
William Morrow and Co., Inc., in a collection entitled *You Be Good & I'll Be Night*.

ISBN 0-440-84939-X

This edition published by arrangement with Henry Holt and Company, Inc.

Printed in the United States of America
March 1993

10 9 8 7 6 5 4 3 2 1
UPR

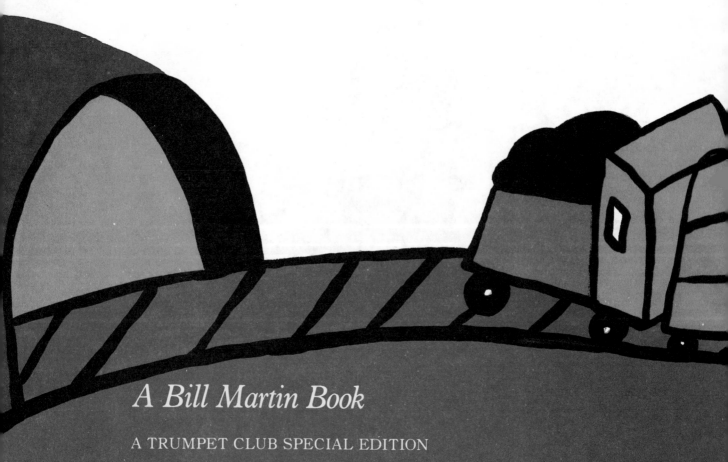

A Bill Martin Book

A TRUMPET CLUB SPECIAL EDITION

EVE MERRIAM

TRAIN LEAVES THE STATION

Illustrated by
DALE GOTTLIEB

1 Hunter on the horse, fox on the run,

train leaves the station at one-o-one.

2 Buckle on the belt, lace in the shoe,

train leaves the station at two-o-two.

3 Worm in the garden, apple on the tree,

train leaves the station at three-o-three.

4

Light on the ceiling, rug on the floor,

train leaves the station at four-o-four.

5 Berry on the bush, honey in the hive,

train leaves the station at five-o-five.

6 Salt in the ocean, clay in the bricks,

train leaves the station at six-o-six.

7

Snake in the grass, angel in heaven,

train leaves the station
at seven-o-seven.

8 Ink in the pen, chalk on the slate,

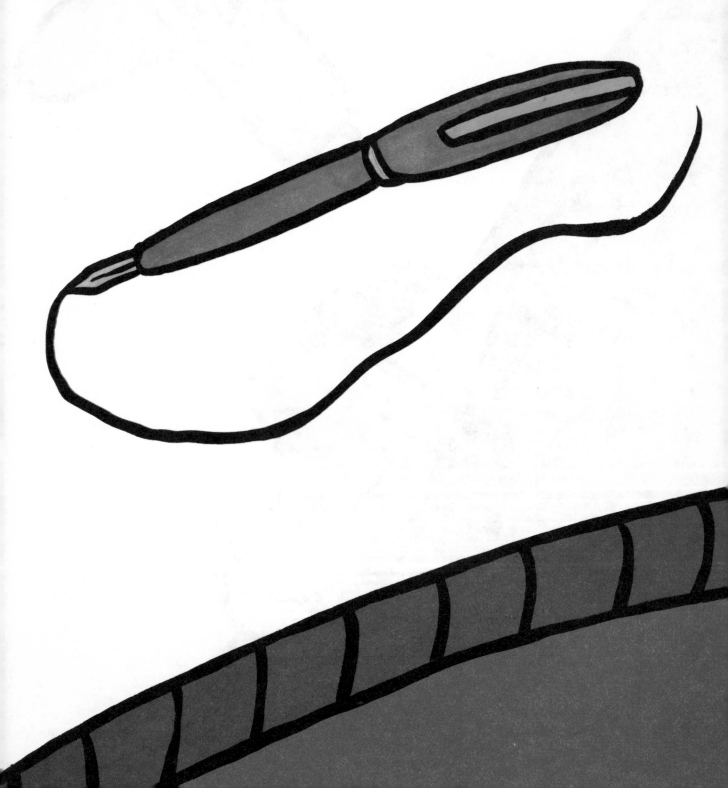

train leaves the station at eight-o-eight.

9

Sand in the desert, coal in the mine,

train leaves the station at nine-o-nine.

Cow in the barn, bear in the den,

train got stuck at the station again.

1

2

3

4

5

6

7

8

9

10